INSECTS FOR KIDS

Bluebottle Fly, page 49

INSECTS FOR KIDS

A JUNIOR SCIENTIST'S GUIDE
to Bees, Butterflies, and Other Flying Insects

SHARMAN JOHNSTON, EdD

ROCKRIDGE PRESS

To my mother, who gave me wings

For general information on our other products and services or to obtain technical support, please contact our Customer Care Department within the United States at (866) 744-2665, or outside the United States at (510) 253-0500.

Rockridge Press publishes its books in a variety of electronic and print formats. Some content that appears in print may not be available in electronic books, and vice versa.

Interior and Cover Designer: Emma Hall
Art Producer: Tom Hood
Editor: Mary Colgan
Production Manager: Jose Olivera
Production Editor: Sigi Nacson

Illustrations @ Kate Francis, 2020. Photographs SPL/Science Source, cover and pp. 30, 31, 52; ephotocorp/Alamy, pp. ii, vi, 42, 44; Barbara Strnadova/Science Source, pp. viii, 1; Richard Becker/Alamy, p. 6; Cindy Sutton/Alamy, p. 16; Gilbert S. Grant/Science Source, pp. 22, 51; Archive PL/Alamy, p. 24; blickwinkel/Alamy, pp. 34, 35, 64, 68, 74, 76, 77; Gilles Mermet/Science Source, p. 36; Nature Collection/Alamy, p. 37; fabio lotti/Alamy, p. 42; Steve Holroyd/Alamy, p. 43; Chuchawan/Shutterstock, p. 45; Nigel Cattlin/Alamy, p. 48; Gordon Zammit/Alamy, p. 50; Natural History Collection/Alamy, pp. 55, 70; David Hansche/Alamy, p. 56; Brian Parker/Alamy, p. 57; Rick and Nora Bowers/Alamy, p. 58; Jim Lane/Alamy, p. 61; Andrew Ammendolia/Alamy, p. 62; Patrick Landmann/Science Source, p. 63; Selfwood/Alamy, p. 69; Scott Camazine/Science Source, p. 71; Kevin Wells/Alamy, p. 75.

ISBN: Print 978-1-64739-352-6
eBook 978-1-64739-353-3

R1

Printed in China

CONTENTS

Luna Moth, page 44

WELCOME, JUNIOR SCIENTIST!

Have you ever wondered why fireflies flash or how crickets chirp? Would you like to know what insect is attracted to smelly feet or which one can lift 850 times its weight? If you like to ask questions and want to know more about the world around you, then you are a junior scientist!

Join me on a journey to explore the buzzing, chirping, creeping-crawling world of insects. These creatures make up Earth's largest group of animals, and they come in almost every shape and color you can imagine. In this book, we'll focus on flying insects and meet some unusual characters, including a prehistoric giant the size of a crow, a mouthless moth, and a beetle that spends its life in poop!

As a junior scientist, you'll not only learn some fascinating facts but will also find many ways to explore these remarkable creatures on your own—by conducting scientific experiments, planting a pollination garden, and more. Let's get started!

Royal Goliath Beetle, page 36

PART ONE

AMAZING INSECTS

No matter where you are, you're never far from an insect. They're crawling in the ground beneath your feet, fluttering in your garden, and even living inside your home. Scientists who study insects are called **entomologists**. Entomologists estimate, or use what they know to guess, that there are about 200 million insects for every human being on Earth.

Try counting the number of ants scurrying around an anthill, and you'll have some idea how challenging it is for scientists to know the exact number of insects in the world. There are many reasons insects are difficult to count.

- They live in every type of **terrestrial**, or land, habitat—from desert valleys to rain forest treetops. There's even one **species** that lives in freezing Antarctica!
- They reproduce, or make babies, extremely fast. Common houseflies lay about 500 eggs in their lifetime (around 21 days). Once those baby flies hatch, they begin laying their own eggs within a few days.
- Insects can be hard to find. *Nanosella fungi*, a species of North American featherwing beetle, is smaller than the period at the end of this sentence. In 2015, scientists discovered an even smaller featherwing, which they named *Scydosella musawasensis.* It can be seen only with a special microscope.

Scientists try to guess how many insects are on Earth by exploring **ecosystems**. They study small areas of a habitat, like a forest, to learn about insects living there. One study in the Amazon rain forest found 700 different species of beetles living on one tree. Scientists take what they learn from a range of studies to help them understand an entire ecosystem—like the Amazon rain forest or the African savanna. So far, entomologists have identified almost a million species of insects. Mammals, the group of animals that we humans belong to, have only 5,500 species.

The First Insects

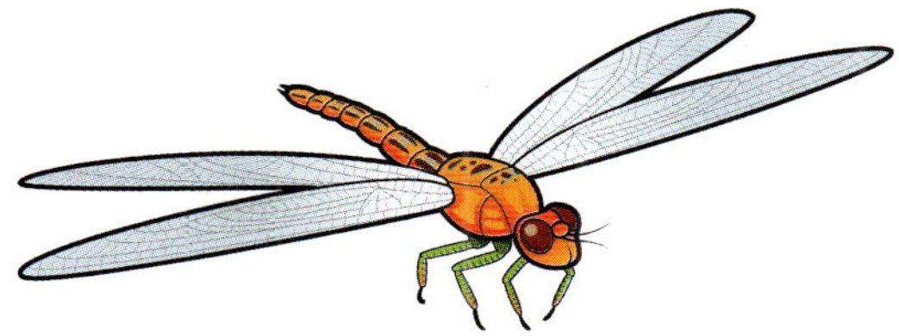

The next time you're bothered by a buzzing fly, just be thankful it's not the size of a crow. The largest insect ever discovered was a prehistoric relative of the dragonfly with wings that stretched 30 inches across. That is about as wide as your refrigerator!

Insects first appeared more than 400 million years ago—long before dinosaurs walked the Earth. Back then, most plants and animals lived in the oceans. When plants began to grow on land, a few **crustaceans** decided to leave the water, becoming the first insects.

The earliest insects did not have wings. It took another 100 million years for insects with wings to appear. Scientists still aren't sure *why* or *how* insects developed wings, but they agree that the ability to fly made insect numbers grow quickly. With flight, insects could explore new habitats, build homes high above **predators**, and find new sources of food.

Compared with insects today, many were enormous. If you're glad you don't have to battle giant cockroaches, you can thank a bird. Why? As more insects appeared, so did new species of flying reptiles. These creatures eventually became birds. They began to hunt the larger insects. Insects needed to find ways to survive, so they slowly evolved, or changed, into the smaller forms we see today.

DID YOU KNOW?

In 2011, scientists who study fossils, called paleontologists, discovered the fossil of a 50-million-year-old ant the size of a hummingbird in Wyoming.

JUNIOR SCIENTISTS IN ACTION

One of the best ways to study insects is to collect some. Collecting insects is as easy as 1, 2, 3! Remember to let them go when you are finished studying them.

1. **Dress for Success**
Protect yourself from accidental stings or bites by wearing a long-sleeved shirt, long pants, socks, and shoes. Bring a magnifying glass, if you have one.

2. **Create a Collection Kit**
Use things from around the house to carefully collect insects:

- **CLEAN PLASTIC OR GLASS CONTAINERS:** Recycle these items into collection jars. You can also fill a glass jar with water and seal it to create a magnifying glass. Hold it above an insect and look through the water.

- **INDEX CARD:** Use a bent index card to scoop up small insects.
- **KITCHEN COLANDER:** Use a colander to collect insects from the surface or along the edges of a pond, lake, or stream.
- **GARDENING TOOLS:** Use a rake to look under leaf piles and a shovel to see what's living beneath the soil.
- **OLD UMBRELLA:** Open the umbrella and turn it upside down beneath a tree or a bush. Give the branches a shake and collect the insects that fall into the umbrella.

3. **Know Where to Look**

Search for dead insects on porches and patios, in your garage, and inside window frames. To find live insects, look around flowers and trees, under rocks or landscaping stones, in sidewalk cracks, and around outdoor lights at night. Once you begin looking, you'll see insects everywhere!

Meet the Insect Class

Plants and animals are divided into groups and named through a method called **taxonomy**. It might help you to think of taxonomy as a ladder. The top rung stands for all life-forms on Earth. With each step down, we get more information about the life-form's description.

Every living thing on Earth can be described using the eight rungs of the taxonomy ladder: domain, kingdom, phylum, class, order, family, genus, and finally, species. The chart on the opposite page shows the taxonomy of *Coccinella septempunctata*. You probably know this insect by its common name: the seven-spotted ladybug.

DOMAIN	EUKARYA	**ALL ANIMALS AND PLANTS -** abcut 2,000,000 species we know of
KINGDOM	ANIMALIA	**ALL ANIMALS -** about 1,260,000 species we know of
PHYLUM	ARTHROPODA	ALL **INVERTEBRATES** WITH AN **EXOSKELETON -** about 1,200,000 species we know of
CLASS	INSECTA	**ALL INSECTS -** about 1,000,000 species we know of
ORDER	COLEOPTERA	**ALL BEETLES -** about 400,000 species we know of
FAMILY	COCCINELLIDAE	**ALL LADYBUGS -** about 5,000 species we know of
GENUS	*COCCINELLA*	**MOSTLY RED-AND-BLACK LADYBUGS -** about 15 species we know of
SPECIES	*COCCINELLA SEPTEMPUNCTATA*	**SEVEN-SPOTTED LADYBUG -** 1 species

Insects, Head to Feet

Insects are cold-blooded invertebrates—animals without spines—that have an exoskeleton instead of bones. Most species hatch from eggs. These things are also true for arachnids (spiders and scorpions) and crustaceans (crabs, shrimp, and lobsters). So, how can you tell if an animal is an insect?

- All insects have three body parts—head, thorax, and abdomen. Their exoskeletons are made of **chitin**. This material is much like the material that forms your fingernails.
  - → An insect's antennae and mouthparts are located on its head.
  - → Legs and wings are connected to the thorax.
  - → The abdomen contains most of the insect's organs. Insect blood, called hemolymph, is clear or greenish yellow. Instead of lungs, insects breathe through openings in their abdomens called pores.
- All insects have two antennae. They are used for feeling and smelling.
- Most insects have six legs. Mosquitoes and roaches use their leg hairs to taste. Butterflies and houseflies taste with their feet.

- Insects have compound eyes. This means that each eye is made up of thousands of tiny lenses. Insects have super vision, because each eye can see many different views, in all different directions. Your eyes each have only one **lens**, so you can see only one set of images at a time. This type of eye is called a simple eye. Adult flying insects usually have three simple eyes located behind their compound eyes.
- Most insects have two pairs of wings.
- Insects have either a **proboscis**, which they use for drinking, or jawlike **mandibles**, which they use for chewing. Bees have both!
- Some species also have body parts that no other insects have. Honeybees, for instance, have three unique parts: pollen combs, pollen baskets, and stingers.
    - → Honeybees gather pollen with their hairy pollen combs.
    - → Bees rub their back legs together to move pollen to the pollen baskets.
    - → Female bees have stingers on their abdomens.

DID YOU KNOW?
Dragonflies have some of the largest eyes in the insect world. Each eye can have 30,000 lenses. That's like having 60,000 eyes!

Wondrous Wings

Of all the animals on Earth, only insects, bats, and birds can fly. (Sorry, flying squirrels! Gliding doesn't count.) There are a few insects without wings, but 99.9 percent of all insects have them. Being able to fly means it's easier to escape danger, travel to new habitats, find new sources of food, and locate mates.

Insect wings are different from those of birds and bats. Except for flies, most insects have four wings instead of two. They are made of the same material as the insect's exoskeleton—chitin. Some wings are covered with scales instead of feathers or skin. Insect wings can be wide or narrow, hard or delicate, straight or twisted, black as night or as colorful as a rainbow.

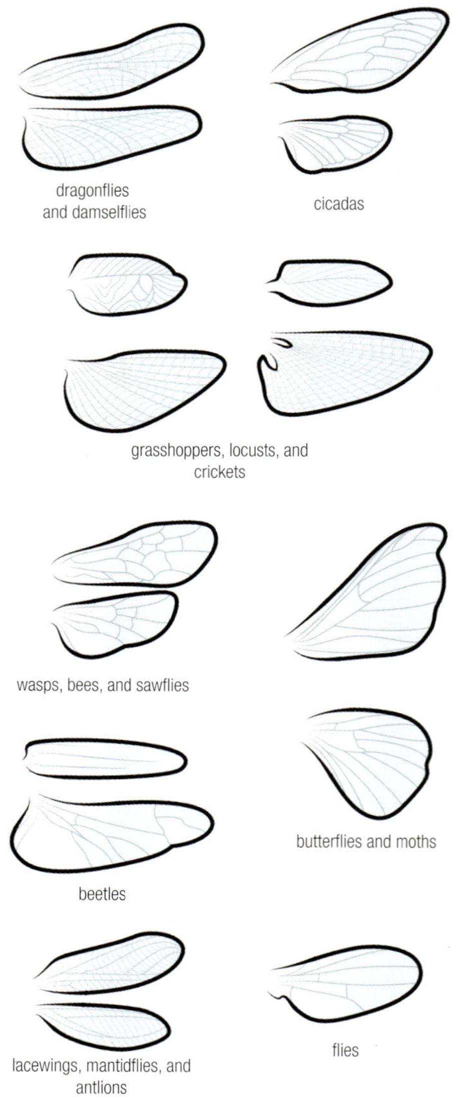

Insects are expert fliers. Try to catch a fly and you'll quickly find that it can zoom by in a blur, turn in midair, hover like a helicopter, or perform a loop the loop. Entomologists know that most insect wings work together as one pair. Until recently, they've been puzzled about how insects are able to pull off their flying stunts.

In 2017, scientists used high-speed cameras to photograph a mosquito in flight. They discovered that it flapped its wings 800 times in a single second! To compare, a hummingbird beats its wings 60 times per second, and a common sparrow can manage only 15 flaps in a second. Birds move their wings up and down, but insects move their wings in a looping movement that looks like the number 8. This motion allows them to make sharp turns and rolls.

DID YOU KNOW?

In 2014, researchers discovered that bees can fly almost as high as airplanes—more than 29,000 feet above the ground.

JUNIOR SCIENTISTS IN ACTION

Use a notebook to keep records of the insects you find. Your insect journal could include a drawing or photo of the insect, its common and scientific names, its habitat (where you found it), its neighbors (plants or animals nearby), and a description (what it looked like and what it was doing).

Use detail in your descriptions. What colors or patterns does the insect have? Is it buzzing, chirping, clicking, or making another sound? How does it move? Is it flying, wiggling, crawling, swimming, or jumping?

If you found your insect on a plant, you could also keep a piece of the plant in your journal. Follow these steps to press and preserve your plants.

1. Pluck a couple of leaves or petals from the plant.
2. Gently brush off any dirt.

3. Dry the plant by placing it between two sheets of parchment paper or two coffee filters.
4. Place your sample between the pages of a heavy book. Then stack a few more books on top.
5. In about a week, remove your dried sample and place it between two sheets of wax paper.
6. Cover the paper with a thin cloth and ask an adult to help you iron it on a low setting.
7. When the wax paper has cooled, trim off the extra paper and add the pressed plant to your journal.

About 80 percent of insects on Earth still have not been identified. Who knows? You might discover a brand-new species!

From Egg to Adult

When you were born, it was easy to tell that you were a human, and not a polar bear, chicken, or sea turtle. But insects develop in stages, or steps. This type of **life cycle** is called **metamorphosis**.

There are two types of insect metamorphosis: complete and simple. A complete metamorphosis has four stages: egg, larva, pupa, and adult. Most insects—including butterflies, moths, flies, ants, bees, and beetles—go through complete metamorphosis. A simple metamorphosis has three stages: egg, nymph, and adult. Dragonflies, cockroaches, grasshoppers, and termites grow this way. The larvae, called nymphs, look like their parents, except they are smaller and don't have wings.

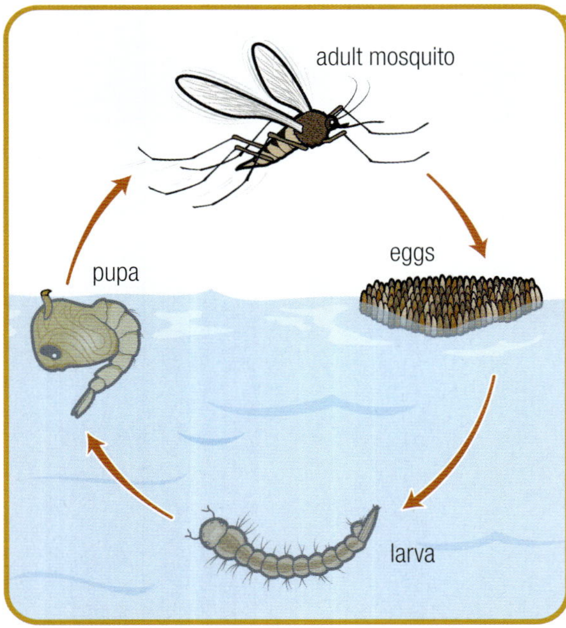

COMPLETE METAMORPHOSIS: MOSQUITO

The mosquito life cycle begins with a raft of eggs floating on top of the water. The eggs hatch into larvae. The larvae, called wigglers, live in water, but they must come to the surface to breathe air. Wigglers turn into pupae called tumblers. Tumblers also float to the surface to breathe air. After a few days, adults burst out of the pupae and rest on the surface of the water until their wings dry and harden. Then they are ready to fly and look for mates.

SIMPLE METAMORPHOSIS: DRAGONFLY

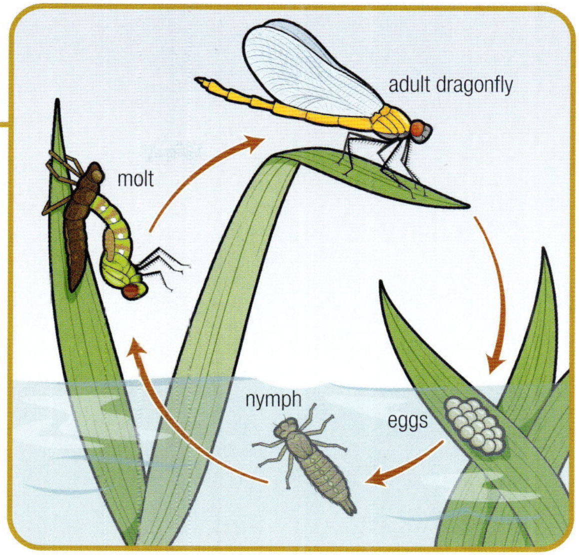

Most dragonfly species lay their eggs on grass, leaves, rotting wood, or other plant materials close to water. The eggs hatch into larvae, called nymphs. Dragonflies spend most of their lives underwater as nymphs, eating and **molting** for as long as five years. When the time is right, the nymph leaves the water; then its back splits and an adult begins to emerge, or come out. The head, thorax, legs, and wings come out first. After about 30 minutes, when the legs have hardened, the abdomen is pulled out. The cycle is complete, and the adult dragonfly is ready to hunt!

DID YOU KNOW?
Frogs, toads, and other amphibians also go through metamorphosis—from water-breathing babies with gills to air-breathing adults with lungs.

FACTS TO DRIVE YOU BUGGY

If you happen to take a winter stroll through northern Canada or Greenland and notice a furry frozen caterpillar, leave it alone. Although it's not moving, the woolly bear caterpillar is probably not dead.

It takes a lot of energy for a caterpillar to spin a **cocoon**, and there isn't a lot of food in those northern places during the winter. Even in the summer, when there is a lot of food, it is still very chilly. Woolly bears spend most of their time trying to stay warm. Once winter comes, they haven't stored enough energy to make a cocoon. The caterpillars hibernate, or "sleep," through the winter. To survive, they make a type of antifreeze that keeps them from freezing solid at temperatures below −70°F.

It can take up to 14 years of hibernating, then eating to store energy, then hibernating again before the woolly bear is able to spin its cocoon. When a woolly bear finally comes out of its cocoon, it has become an Isabella tiger moth. After all that work, the moth lives less than a week—just long enough to mate and lay eggs.

Isabella tiger moths and their woolly bear larvae are common throughout North America, which makes you wonder . . . *How did some woolly bears end up in the chilly Arctic whereas others live in sunny Florida?*

Beginning Again

Many insects must find a mate before they can reproduce. For some species, it's a matter of being the first to find a mate. Male mosquitoes, for example, become adults before the females do. The males simply wait by a female's pupal case until she comes out. Males of certain beetles, wasps, bees, and other insects gather in large groups called leks to search for a mate. Other insects need to be a little more creative to find a partner.

Pheromones are chemical scents made by many insect species. Females make pheromones that attract males. Male silkworm moths have sometimes traveled 30 miles while following the scent trail of a female. But following pheromones can be tricky. Bolas spiders, for example, can copy the pheromones of some moths. A moth might think it's following a potential mate, only to find a hungry spider ready to eat it!

Butterflies and houseflies use their sense of sight to look for clues that a mate could be near. So do fireflies. These summer insects are famous for their flashing lights. But why do they flash? Females blink specific codes when they're ready to mate. Males reply back with their own codes. They will both keep flashing until they've found each other.

Many females mate with the first male that comes by, but some species have courtship rituals. These are things a male does to impress the female so she'll mate with him. These rituals can include songs, dances, and even gifts. Male balloon flies bring females gifts of silken balloons. For female scorpion flies, nothing says love like a big ball of spit! Males make dripping blobs of saliva. The largest blobs are the ones most likely to impress a female.

Scientists are still learning how insect eggs develop in the female's body after they are fertilized by the male. One thing is certain. The eggs pop out in a dazzling assortment of sizes, colors, and shapes. They can be round, oval, or barrel-shaped and have stripes, spots, or spikes. Some species, like mantises and cockroaches, protect their eggs with a hard casing called an **ootheca**. A single mantis ootheca can contain hundreds of eggs.

DID YOU KNOW?
Photuris fireflies are predatory, which means they hunt other insects. The females copy the female signals of other firefly species and eat the males that show up.

Let's Chat . . . About Insect Communication

A human infant communicates by crying and moving its body because it can't speak words. Humans have to learn how to speak, but most animals do not. Every insect is born with a special language that allows it to communicate with other members of its species.

Insects share information for many reasons:

- to recognize their relatives and nest mates
- to warn other insects if danger is near
- to give directions to food or other resources
- to defend their territory
- to confuse predators

There are four kinds of insect communication—smell, touch, sound, and sight.

SMELL

Pheromones are the most important form of communication. Although these chemicals are made mostly for mating, insects also use other types of smells. Ants play Follow the Leader by leaving a scent trail that keeps the **colony** walking in a straight line. Amazonian slave-maker ants produce pheromones that spell doom for the colonies of other ant species. They spray them with a chemical that causes the ants inside to become confused. Then they swoop in and steal the colony's larvae.

TOUCH

When it comes to dancing, no one boogies like a bee! The well-known honeybee waggle dance is an example of communicating through touch. Bee dances tell other honeybees where to find food. Since the dances are performed inside the dark hive, bees can't see the fancy dance moves. Instead, they feel the vibrations on the honeycomb—the same way you can feel the vibrations caused by someone stomping on the floor.

SOUND

Insects usually make sounds to find a mate or to warn off predators, but do you wonder how they hear? Insect ears can be located almost anywhere, including on their antennae, legs, or abdomens. Cicadas win the medal for loudest insect. Their calls can reach 120 decibels, which is as loud as thunder, and can be heard a mile or more away.

SIGHT

Fireflies aren't the only insects that glow. A tropical click beetle has two "headlights" and another light on its abdomen. The lights are normally a soft blue-green glow, but click beetles can make them shine brighter to scare off predators. The "headlights" look like a pair of eyes that frighten predators.

DID YOU KNOW?

A honeybee's waggle dance tells other worker bees how far a food source is from the nest and in which direction to fly to find it. The longer she "waggles," the farther the food!

Insects Near and Far

They're small, have fragile bodies, and are near the bottom of the food chain. So how did insects become the largest group of animals on the planet? There are many reasons. Let's explore a few!

Insects can live in almost every habitat on Earth. Most animal species prefer one kind of habitat. Kangaroos are a good example. Unless you live in Australia, you're not likely to find one in your backyard. However, a single insect species may live in many different habitats. For example, the Argentine ant was first found in tropical parts of South America, but it has spread across the globe to forests, fields, coastal plains, and tropical islands.

Termite colony

Some insects live in more than one habitat throughout their lives. Dragonflies spend many years underwater before taking to the air. Cicadas live underground for up to 17 years as larvae before climbing a tree to become a chirping, flying insect.

They're not picky eaters. About half of all insects eat plants, and some eat other animals. Bedbugs and ticks are bloodsuckers, and dung beetles eat poop!

They lay a LOT of eggs. Some insects lay fewer than 10 eggs, but most lay anywhere from 100 to 1,000 eggs at a time. One Australian ghost moth can lay 30,000 eggs. An African driver ant queen can lay more than a million eggs in a month. That's a lot of babies!

Bigger isn't always better. Big animals have BIG appetites. An elephant can eat up to 600 pounds of food and drink a bathtub full of water in a day. That amount of food could be hard to find. An ant, on the other hand, can survive on a few crumbs of your pizza and a drop of water. It's also hard to hide an elephant, but an ant can hide from predators in the crack of a sidewalk or underneath a pebble.

They're smarter than you think. Some insects—like bees, ants, and termites—build complicated societies called colonies. They communicate, cooperate, and even divide up the chores. Some feed the babies, whereas others get the groceries or take out the trash. They're a lot like your own family, if you had a few thousand brothers and sisters!

DID YOU KNOW?

Cockroaches can live two to three months without food, and a month without water.

FACTS TO DRIVE YOU BUGGY

Would you eat an insect? More than two billion people around the world do. They are called entomophagists, and they regularly eat protein-packed, fiber-filled insects. Here's a look at just a few of the many insect dishes on the menu in many African, Asian, and Latin American countries.

Beondegi

- *Beondegi* is a Korean street food made with silkworm pupae. The pupae are boiled or steamed to bring out the slightly fishy, nutty flavor, and they are served in paper cups.
- *The Jumil Festival* in Mexico honors the lowly stinkbug, which is eaten both alive and cooked. Ancient tribes believed that the bugs could cure sickness.

- *Insect food carts* in Thailand offer dozens of choices. Many people say the fried cricket snacks, called *Jing Leed*, taste like popcorn.
- *Chapulines* are roasted grasshoppers, seasoned with chili powder and lime, that are served in many parts of Mexico.
- If you're offered a raisin-filled cookie in Japan, look carefully. Those "raisins" might actually be digger wasps. Crackers made of wasps and rice flour are popular treats in many parts of Japan.

Which dish would you like to try?

The Good Guys

It's safe to say that no one wants a home filled with mosquitoes, flies, or bedbugs, but these common pests are only a small number of the world's insect species. In many ways, our ecosystems couldn't survive without our tiny neighbors.

POWERFUL POLLINATORS

Imagine a world where more than half of our flowers, grasses, and trees disappeared. Flowering plants must be **pollinated** to produce seeds and fruit. More than three-fourths of all plants have flowers, and 80 percent are pollinated by insects. Butterflies and bees are the best-known pollinators, but they aren't the only ones. Without a particular species of the tiny flies called midges, there would be no chocolate. They are the only cacao tree pollinators.

THE FOOD CHAIN

Insects are the only source of food for many birds, reptiles, amphibians, and other types of animals. Insects and their young are also important **decomposers**. They break down rotting plant and animal matter and return nutrients to the soil. Without insects, we'd be up to our elbows in leaves and dead animals!

SOIL SUPERSTARS

Healthy soil is about 50 percent air. Air pockets, or spaces, carry water throughout the soil and give roots room to grow. Burrowing insects, such as ants and beetles, keep the soil from becoming too packed, which helps plant roots grow deep. When insects die, their bodies add nutrients to the soil. Insect poop, called frass, is an amazing fertilizer that provides food for plants.

FARMER'S FRIENDS

Some insects, like aphids and whiteflies, can damage or kill plants. Farmers and gardeners sometimes collect or buy predatory insects to get rid of these pests. Ladybugs, praying mantises, green lacewings, and other insects are more than happy to snack on the pests and save crops.

DID YOU KNOW?
Tortoise beetle larvae carry frass on their backs to camouflage themselves from predators.

JUNIOR SCIENTISTS IN ACTION

Create a nature garden in your own backyard where you can observe butterflies and other pollinators at work. Just follow these simple steps:

- **SELECT A PLACE TO PLANT.** Your plants will need plenty of sunshine and protection from strong winds. They will need good soil that is at least 10 inches deep.
- **CHOOSE PLANTS THAT NATURALLY GROW IN YOUR AREA.** These plants will attract more insects that live near you. They will also be easier to take care of. The National Wildlife Foundation website has a great tool for learning about the plants and butterflies in your area. Find it at: nwf.org/NativePlantFinder.
- **INCLUDE PLANTS FOR BUTTERFLIES AND THEIR CATERPILLARS.** Butterflies are attracted to nectar, but if you want them to stay in your garden, you'll need plants for their caterpillars to munch. Nectar plants for adults are usually different from the plants their larvae need to eat.

- **AVOID PESTICIDES.** Pesticides kill insects. Sprays that kill mosquitoes and other pests will also kill ladybugs, butterflies, and bees.

- **PROVIDE A PUDDLE CLUB.** Butterflies need water, but they don't really like large amounts of water, like ponds and birdbaths. Many species like to gather around moist sand or mud. The puddles provide them with moisture and minerals from the soil. Attract a "puddle club" of butterflies to your yard by filling a clay saucer (or similar shallow container) with sand or gravel. Bury it in the ground to the rim, and add water.

- **ROCK ON!** Add a large, flat rock to give butterflies a place where they can bask in the early morning sun.

Oblong-Winged Katydid, page 70

PART TWO

INSECTS UP CLOSE

So now that you know what an insect is, are you ready to meet some six-legged friends from around the world? In this part of the book, we will explore seven of the largest orders of insects. Some might be living in your house or garden right now. Others may live thousands of miles away.

You will begin your tour of the insect kingdom with the beetles. Almost half of all insects come from this group! Then keep reading to learn about a moth with no mouth, a wasp that makes its house out of mud, and a cricket that can tell the temperature!

Coleoptera: Beetles

Trying to count the number of beetles on Earth would be like trying to count the stars in the sky or the grains of sand on a beach. The Coleoptera order is so large that 25 percent of *all* life-forms on Earth are beetles. Beetles come in many different forms—from lovable ladybugs and flickering fireflies to fist-sized giants and crop-destroying invaders.

Beetles also come in all sizes. Some featherwing beetles are so small that you would need a microscope to see them. Others are huge. The titan beetle grows to be 6.5 inches long and has jaws so strong it can snap a pencil in half.

Instead of sipping nectar, beetles use mouthparts called mandibles to cut or crush their food—and some species can cause a lot of damage. Boll weevils feed on cotton plants and can ruin an entire crop. The larvae of pine and bark beetles chew their way into trees and destroy entire forests.

Like most insects, beetles have two pairs of wings. The hard front wings, called elytra, are made of the same chitin as the beetles' exoskeletons. The elytra protect the second pair of wings below.

About 10 percent of Coleoptera can't fly, and many of these species have wings that do special things. The Namib Desert beetle's wings are covered in bumps that collect moisture from the air. When the beetle gets thirsty, it stands on its head so the water droplets flow into its mouth. Other species trap air beneath their wings so they can hunt underwater. An ironclad beetle's wings are joined together to create a shield so strong that almost nothing can eat it. This beetle can even survive being stepped on!

In addition to super-hard shells, many other defenses serve beetles well against predators. Some roll over and play dead. Others, like male rhinoceros and Hercules beetles, have long horns that are used for fighting. Many ladybug species release a sticky yellow substance that gums up the antennae and mouthparts of attackers. The Australian tiger beetle, one of the world's speediest insects, runs so fast that everything around it becomes a blur. It must stop every few seconds to see where it is!

Between armor, biting jaws, and other **adaptations**, it's no wonder that beetles live in every kind of habitat—from the frozen Arctic tundra to the blistering heat of the Sahara Desert to the treetops of the Amazon rain forest.

Bombardier Beetles

Brachinus

SAY IT! *BRAK-ih-nus*

Bombardiers are a group of 500 ground beetle species that are found on every continent except Antarctica. They are nocturnal, which means they are active only at night. In the air force, a bombardier is the person on a warplane who drops bombs. These beetles live up to their name. A bombardier beetle's abdomen contains two chemical chambers. When the beetle feels threatened, it mixes the chemicals together and they explode with a *POP!* The boiling hot, toxic spray sends predators running.

INSECT STATS

Habitat

Grasslands, forests, and wetlands throughout the world

Length

½ to 1 inch

Color/Pattern

Blue-black elytra, with red antennae, head, thorax, and legs

Diet

Smaller insects and other **arthropods**

Life Span

Several weeks

Common Whirligig Beetle

Gyrinus natator

SAY IT! *JYE-rye-nus NA-ta-tor*

More than 900 species of whirligig water beetles are found in rivers, streams, and ponds around the world. These little beetles swim in fast swirling patterns and make a rotten-apple smell to confuse and drive away predators. Whirligigs are unique because they have two pairs of compound eyes. One pair sees above the surface of the water, and the other pair looks beneath the water.

INSECT STATS

Habitat

Rivers, streams, and ponds throughout the world

Length

¼ inch

Color/Pattern

Shiny black, with reddish legs

Diet

Water fleas and other tiny invertebrates

Life Span

2 to 3 years

Royal Goliath Beetle

Goliathus regius

SAY IT! *Goh-LIE-ah-thus REE-jee-us*

There are five Goliath beetle species. As their name suggests, these are giant insects—about the size of your fist! Goliaths are famous for their strength. They can lift 850 times their weight, which is the same as a 200-pound man lifting more than 40 cars at once! Some people keep these beetles as pets. They will eat any protein-rich dog or cat food.

INSECT STATS

Habitat

Rain forests of western Africa

Length

Up to 4 inches

Color/Pattern

Mostly black, with streaks of white on the thorax and elytra

Diet

Fruit, bark, and tree sap

Life Span

About 3 months in the wild or nearly 1 year in captivity

Rainbow Scarab

Phanaeus vindex

SAY IT! *FAN-ee-us VIN-deks*

The 8,000 species of dung beetles are divided into three groups: tunnelers, rollers, and dwellers. Rainbow scarabs are tunnelers, so they make a tunnel beneath a pile of dung and drag the poop inside. The larvae eat the dung until they become pupae. Rollers create balls of poop, which they bury for later use. Dwellers lay their eggs right inside the dung pile. The larvae hatch and stay there, eating the dung, until they become adults.

INSECT STATS

Habitat	Diet
Grasslands and forests of North America	Dung (poop!)
Length	**Life Span**
½ to 1 inch	Unknown, but rainbow scarabs studied in laboratories have lived up to 1 year
Color/Pattern	
Metallic shades of blue, green, and red; golden head with yellow antennae and a black horn (on males) that curves from the head back to the thorax	

Lepidoptera: Butterflies and Moths

With their bright colors and detailed wing designs, lepidopterans are the supermodels of the insect world. There are about 160,000 species of moths and 20,000 species of butterflies, making Lepidoptera the second-largest order, after Coleoptera. The name Lepidoptera comes from two Greek words: *lepis*, meaning "scale," and *ptera*, meaning "wing."

Lepidopterans go through a complete metamorphosis. Their larvae are called caterpillars. Adults are covered in scales made of chitin. These scales may be wide and flat or thin and hairlike. Their tiny wing scales overlap, like shingles on a roof. If you touch a butterfly or a moth, the scales will come off, leaving a dusty powder on your finger.

Although lepidopterans lose wing scales throughout their lives, they will die if their wings are broken. The good news is that lepidopteran wings are much stronger than they look. Butterflies and moths start with wet, shriveled wings. After pumping hemolymph through their wing veins, they hang upside down to let their wings dry and stiffen. Lepidopteran wings can last for thousands of miles. This is beneficial to species like painted ladies and monarchs that make long trips as they **migrate** in search of food or warmer climates.

What do you picture when you hear the word "butterfly"? Do you see its colorful wings? It's true that most butterflies are brightly colored, but nature is full of surprises. There are many brown and tan species of butterflies. There are also bright lime green and royal blue moths. Use the chart on the opposite page to help you tell the difference between butterflies and moths.

	BUTTERFLY	MOTH
Antennae	Long, thin, and club-shaped	Feathery or saw-edged
Pupa	Hard, smooth **chrysalis**	Fuzzy silk cocoon
Body Shape	Thin and smooth	Thick and fuzzy
Resting Wing Position	Vertical (straight up and down)	Horizontal (across like an airplane)
Behavior	Usually diurnal (active during the day)	Usually nocturnal (active at night)
Appearance	Usually brightly colored	Usually dull colored

What if you see a lepidopteran with a dull brown color and a thick, fuzzy body like a moth that is also resting its wings vertically and has clubbed antennae? You've found a skipper! Skippers are a third type of lepidopteran. They share things in common with both butterflies and moths.

Although they prefer to dwell where it's warm, lepidopterans live in every country on Earth. Which country has the most butterfly species? Peru! About one-fourth of all butterfly species can be found there.

DID YOU KNOW?
Lepidopterans smell with their antennae and taste with their feet, and some moths hear with their stomachs.

JUNIOR SCIENTISTS IN ACTION

When lepidopterans are larvae, they have chewing mouthparts with which to eat plants. Adult butterflies and moths have a different mouth-part—a proboscis. Scientists once thought that the pro-boscis was used like a straw to suck up flower nectar, fruit juices, or nutrient-rich water from soil. Today we know that the proboscis acts more like a paper towel than a straw. How does it work?

Sphinx moth drinking nectar

TEST IT

Add a few drops of food col-oring to a half glass of water. Roll a piece of paper towel into a tight tube. Place one end of the paper in the colored water. What happens? The paper towel absorbs the water, and it moves up the tube. Absorb-ing the water works much better for a lepidopteran than drinking it through a straw. If a proboscis worked like a straw, then a butterfly drinking nectar would also suck up bits of pollen and other plant parts. Over time, these solid bits would clog the feeding tube.

DRINK LIKE A SPHINX

The 2.5-inch-long Morgan's sphinx moth has a proboscis that can be an amazing 13 inches long. Can you imagine how hard it would be to drink through such a long straw? Multiply your height by five. That's how long your proboscis would be if you were a sphinx moth!

Common Crow Butterfly

Euploea core

SAY IT! *YOU-plee-ah KOHR*

During mating season, male common crow butterflies stretch yellow-orange brushes from their abdomens and release a scent to attract females. Common crows are members of the Nymphalidae family. They have been nicknamed "brush-footed" or "four-legged" butterflies because their front legs are so small.

INSECT STATS

Habitat	Diet
Tropical areas of India, Asia, and Australia	Flower nectar, including from ficus figs and eucalyptus trees
Wingspan	**Life Span**
2½ to 3 inches	**ADULT:** 11 to 13 weeks
Color/Pattern	
Black-brown wings, with white spots on the borders of the front and back wings	

Hummingbird Hawk-Moth

Macroglossum stellatarum

SAY IT! *Ma-kroh-GLAH-sum stel-lah-TAR-um*

All hummingbird moths have bodies covered with hairlike scales that are almost like feathers. This species is active during the day. It hovers when sipping nectar, and even makes a humming sound with its rapidly beating wings. A hummingbird hawk's wings are so strong that it can even fly and feed when it's raining.

INSECT STATS

Habitat

Meadows and woodlands in southern Europe, North Africa, and Asia

Wingspan

About 2 inches

Color/Pattern

Orange-brown back wings, with gray front wings; black-and-white checkered body

Diet

LARVA: Mostly bedstraw plants

ADULT: Flower nectar from dianthus, verbena, and honeysuckle flowers

Life Span

LARVA: 3 to 4 weeks

PUPA: 3 weeks

ADULT: 6 to 7 months

Luna Moth

Actias luna

SAY IT! *AK-tee-us LOO-nah*

Unlike other lepidopterans, luna moths spend most of their lives in the larva and pupa stages. Why? Because the adults don't have mouths! Adult lunas have no proboscises or digestive systems. Without food, they live only long enough to find a mate and reproduce.

INSECT STATS

Habitat

Forests of the eastern United States and southern Canada

Wingspan

4 to 5 inches

Color/Pattern

Bright green wings with long tails; the front wings have purple-gray edges; the back wings have two round white markings, called eyespots

Diet

LARVA: Walnut, hickory, sweet gum, and other deciduous tree leaves

ADULT: Nothing

Life Span

LARVA: 1 month

PUPA: 3 weeks

ADULT: 5 to 7 days

Monarch Butterfly

Danaus plexippus

SAY IT! *DAN-ay-us PLEX-ih-pus*

Monarchs born in April through July complete their life cycles in about four weeks. But the ones born in August are different. Late-summer monarchs spend all their time eating. They are storing energy for a journey of up to 3,000 miles that will take them to their winter homes in central Mexico. They will not reproduce until they return in the spring.

INSECT STATS

Habitat

Open fields and forests of North and South America

Wingspan

3 to 4 inches

Color/Pattern

Dark orange wings, with black veins and borders dotted with white spots

Diet

LARVA: Milkweed only

ADULT: Nectar from flowers such as milkweed, goldenrod, and thistles

Life Span

LARVA: 2 weeks

PUPA: About 10 days

ADULT: 2 to 6 weeks

MIGRATING ADULT: 6 to 8 months

Diptera: Flies, Flies, Flies!

Flies, gnats, and mosquitoes are all members of Diptera, the third-largest insect order. Scientists call the 150,000 dipteran species "true flies," because they are very different from butterflies, dragonflies, and other insects with "fly" in their names.

Diptera means "two wings," and dipterans have two large front wings and two short back wings called halteres. The halteres look like tiny drumsticks and help these flies keep their balance. During flight, the halteres vibrate up and down, keeping time with the wings. True flies also have compound eyes so large that they can see what's behind them without turning around.

Flies have eating habits that are far worse than talking with your mouth full. Take the common housefly. When a housefly lands on your cupcake, it uses its feet to taste it. Then it loosens up some crumbs by scrubbing your cake with the tiny bristles on the end of its proboscis. After that, it throws up! A fly can eat only liquids, so it vomits a mixture of spit and digestive juices on solid foods to make them soupy. The last thing it does is poop. As if throwing up and pooping on your food isn't bad enough, houseflies can also spread harmful bacteria and diseases. Flies eat everything from the rotten food in your garbage can to poop. Their legs pick up tons of germs.

Can you guess the most dangerous animal on Earth? Well, it isn't a great white shark, crocodile, or poisonous snake. It's a mosquito! All adult mosquitoes feed on nectar. For adult female mosquitoes, however, there's more to the story. In order to make eggs, females need protein—which they get from blood. Although we call them mosquito "bites," dipterans don't have teeth. When a female "bites," she is poking a hole in our skin with her needle-sharp proboscis. Although most mosquito bites are harmless, the saliva of some mosquitoes can carry serious diseases, like malaria, especially in tropical places.

Houseflies and mosquitoes give dipterans a bad reputation, but most species help keep our planet healthy. True flies are pollinators for many plants. They are also a source of food for frogs, birds, and other animals. Larvae of species like hoverflies feed on aphids and other garden pests. Dipteran larvae, called maggots, are important decomposers.

True flies can survive in conditions that would kill other insects. *Belgica antarctica*, a tiny wingless midge, is the only insect that lives on our coldest continent. Some flies can live in bubbling hot springs that can be more than 100°F and in water three times saltier than seawater. No matter where you travel, there's probably a fly nearby.

DID YOU KNOW?
Flies have a sticky substance on their feet that allows them to walk on glass and even cling to ceilings.

DID YOU KNOW?
The biting midges are nicknamed "no-see-ums" because they are so small that they seem invisible. Some species are small enough to fly through the openings of a window screen.

FACTS TO DRIVE YOU BUGGY

Dogs, monkeys, rabbits, and mice have all flown into space, but the very first animal astronaut was a fruit fly. In 1947, American scientists launched a rocket filled with fruit flies. The fruit flies flew almost 70 miles into space before parachuting to the ground. When the capsule was opened, the fruit flies were still alive and well.

Fruit flies are small and don't weigh much. This made them the perfect passengers, but there was a more important reason scientists chose them.

Humans and fruit flies are surprisingly alike. More than half of a fruit fly's 14,000 **genes** are also found in humans. Astronaut scientists on the International Space Station study fruit flies to learn about the effects of long-term space flight on humans.

Bluebottle Fly

Calliphora vomitoria

SAY IT! *Cal-i-FOR-ah vah-mih-TOHR-ih-ah*

Any animal that has "vomit" in its name can't be good. Adult bluebottle flies are attracted to anything that smells gross. They pollinate strong-smelling plants like skunk cabbage, and they lay their eggs on dead animals, dung, and garbage. An adult can fly 300 times its length in a single second. That's like a football player running the length of six football fields.

INSECT STATS

Habitat

Any habitat that contains rotting animals in the Northern Hemisphere or in parts of South America and Africa

Color/Pattern

Dark gray head with large red eyes; metallic blue thorax, with black legs and clear wings

Length

About ½ inch, slightly larger than a common **HOUSEFLY**

Diet

LARVA: Dead animals or poop

ADULT: Nectar

Life Span

About 6 weeks

Asian Tiger Mosquito

Aedes albopictus

SAY IT! *Ay-EE-dees al-boh-PIK-tuhs*

In the 1980s, this native Asian species hitched a ride in shipments of used tires and "lucky" bamboo and quickly spread across the globe. Asian tiger mosquito eggs don't need a lot of water. They can hatch in flowerpots, old tires, or soda cans. Unlike most mosquito species, Asian tigers feed all day long instead of just at dawn and dusk. They have also adapted to live in a variety of habitats—especially ones that have humans nearby!

INSECT STATS

Habitat	Diet
Variety of places around the world	Prefers the blood of humans and other mammals

Length	Life Span
Less than ¼ inch	About 3 weeks

Color/Pattern
Black, with silvery white markings and a white stripe running down the center of the head and back

Stalk-Eyed Fly

Teleopsis pallifacies

SAY IT! *Tel-ee-OP-sis pal-ih-FAY-seez*

Those aren't red-tipped antennae that you see on this fly's head. They're eyes! Stalk-eyed flies have their eyes located on two long stalks near their antennae. Female stalks are short, but a male's eyespan can be wider than the length of its entire body. The widest stalks attract more females, but they also make it more difficult to fly. Males have adapted by developing larger wings.

INSECT STATS

Habitat

On low plants near ponds, lakes, rivers, and marshes in southern Asia

Diet

Bacteria and fungi from decaying plants

Length

Less than ½ inch

Life Span

About 2 months

Color/Pattern

Triangular head with two long eyestalks; narrow waist, a bulb-shaped abdomen

Striped Horsefly

Tabanus lineola

SAY IT! *Tah-BAN-us lin-ee-OH-lah*

Like a mosquito, the female striped horsefly, also called a greenhead, needs blood to make her eggs. Instead of piercing the skin with a needlelike proboscis, horseflies use razor-sharp mouthparts that cut into the skin. They can fly up to 30 miles per hour and are often found on Atlantic and Gulf Coast beaches.

INSECT STATS

Habitat	Diet
Coastal plains and wetlands of the United States and Canada	Blood from horses and other animals, as well as humans

Length	Life Span
More than ½ inch—twice the size of a common housefly	1 to 2 weeks

Color/Pattern
Bright green eyes, with a purple stripe across them

Hymenoptera: Bees, Wasps, and Other Stingers

Now let's talk about stinging things with wings. Hymenoptera is the only order with stinging insects, but only 20 percent of the 150,000 species have stingers. Stinging insects are usually social and live together in colonies. Most will sting only when their homes are threatened.

Are you living next to royalty? Insect colonies are built around the queen bee, wasp, or ant. The queen is larger than the others, and her only job is to lay eggs. Males are called drones, and their only job is to mate with the queen. Females are called workers for good reasons. They gather food, feed the larvae, have stingers they can use to protect the nest, and perform housekeeping chores.

Unlike most bees and ants, social wasps are very aggressive. They are always ready to fight, and it doesn't take much to make them attack. Yellow jackets and hornets will not only attack but they'll also call their friends to join in! These wasps send out a special pheromone that makes nearby colony members go on a stinging frenzy. Thankfully, there are also wasp species that live alone and use their stingers only for hunting.

NOTICE: Insect stings can cause dangerous allergic reactions in some people. Always tell an adult if you've been stung.

Scientists group hymenopterans by their wings, not their stingers. Bees, wasps, and winged ants often look like they have only two wings, because their front and back wings are attached together with hooks called hamuli. In the air, their connected wings flap together. This makes them powerful fliers.

Although we mostly see black-and-yellow honeybees and yellow jackets bee and wasp species come in many amazing colors. There are purple carpenter bees, green orchid bees, orange-and-blue hawk wasps, and metallic blue mud daubers. Even bees' honey can be different colors. In 2014, beekeepers in the South of France were shocked to find that their bees had produced blue and green honey. They discovered that the bees had snacked on leftover M&M's candy shells from a nearby factory. The dye colored the honey the same way the candy can color your tongue!

Any place that has flowering plants can be home for bees and wasps. Although they prefer warm climates, many species have adapted to live in cooler places. Honeybees, for example, make heat in their hive by shivering. This keeps the hive at a summery 90 to 95°F, even if it's cold outside. Ants are also found on every continent, except Antarctica. The largest colonies are usually located in warm tropical places.

DID YOU KNOW?
Scientists studying alpine bees discovered that they could fly more than 5.5 miles above the ground—higher than the top of Mount Everest.

Horntail (or Wood Wasp)

Siricidae

SAY IT! *Sigh-rih-SIGH-day*

That wicked-looking "stinger" is actually a drill the female horntail uses to make a hole in wood and lay her eggs. Although they are harmless to humans, the 100 or so species of horntails can cause a lot of damage to trees. Larvae eat the wood, leaving trails of sawdust and frass.

INSECT STATS

Habitat	Diet
Forests in the Northern Hemisphere	Wood
Length	**Life Span**
Up to 1½ inches	**LARVA:** Up to 3 years, depending on the species **ADULT:** Several months
Color/Pattern	
Thick black, dark blue, or rusty-red bodies with no thin "wasp waist" and yellow or white stripes; spines on the tip of the abdomen (males have one, females have two)	

Japanese Honeybee

Apis cerana japonica

SAY IT! *A-pis seh-RAN-ah juh-PAH-nih-kah*

Giant hornets prey on Japanese honeybees. They enter the bees' hive, where each can kill 40 bees in less than a minute. Since Japanese honeybee stingers are no match for an insect four times their size, they have developed a unique way of getting rid of hornet invaders. When a hornet scout enters the nest, the bees swarm around it, creating a bee ball. They vibrate their wings and raise the temperature in the ball to 117°F, which slowly cooks the hornet alive!

INSECT STATS

Habitat	Diet
Variety of habitats throughout Japan	Pollen, nectar
Length	**Life Span**
About ½ inch	**QUEEN:** 2 to 3 years **WORKER:** About 6 weeks
Color/Pattern	
Black head and thorax; yellow-and-black striped abdomen	

Black-and-Yellow Mud Dauber (or Dirt Dobber)

Sceliphron caementarium

SAY IT! *SEL-ih-fron see-men-TAIR-ih-um*

There are several species of mud dauber wasps, and they all build nests made out of mud. They are not social and live alone, but one female may build many nests. Black-and-yellow mud dauber nests are made up of 15 to 20 separate tubelike cells. The female uses her stinger to paralyze spiders. She puts 20 to 30 spiders in each cell and lays a single egg on top.

INSECT STATS

Habitat

Worldwide near man-made structures with a source of mud nearby, but mostly located in the U.S. and Mexico

Length

1 inch or less

Color/Pattern

Black body with yellow stripes; long, skinny "waist"

Diet

LARVA: Spiders

ADULT: Flower nectar

Life Span

About 9 months

Tarantula Hawk Wasp

Pepsis grossa

SAY IT! *PEP-sis GRAH-suh*

If you are a tarantula, there are few things scarier than a tarantula hawk wasp—the state insect of New Mexico. The female of this species uses her stinger to paralyze a tarantula. Then she lays an egg in its abdomen, drags it to a hole, and buries it alive. When the egg hatches, the larva eats the spider. It eats the spider's organs last so that it will stay alive as long as possible.

INSECT STATS

Habitat

Deserts in the southern United States and northern South America

Diet

LARVA: Tarantula spiders
ADULT: Nectar

Length

2 inches

Life Span

About 2 months

Color/Pattern

Shiny blue-black body with orange wings

Hemiptera: The True Bugs

If you were to buy a bag of plastic toys labeled "Bugs," it might contain spiders, centipedes, and scorpions, as well as insects. That's because we often use the word "bug" for any small arthropod. When entomologists talk about bugs, they're referring to aphids, cicadas, stinkbugs, and the other 80,000 species of Hemiptera—nicknamed "true bugs."

The name Hemiptera means "half-wing" in Greek. True bugs have an unusual wing design. Their front wings are hard, like a beetle's wings, but they are clear on the ends. Their back wings are also clear, which makes it look like they have only half-wings. Hemipterans also have a proboscis that is like a beak with a sharp pointed tip. The proboscis has two tubes: One tube puts saliva into a plant or animal to dissolve the tissue there, or make it soupy. The other is used like a straw to suck up the liquid.

True bugs come in all shapes, sizes, and colors, and many have unusual adaptations. The two largest species, *Lethocerus grandis* and *Lethocerus maximus*, are giant 5-inch-long South American water bugs that go snorkeling when looking for a meal. These hunters breathe through special stomach tubes while they hang upside down from underwater plants and wait for prey to swim by. They are big and strong enough to gobble up fish, ducklings, turtles, and even poisonous snakes!

Several true bug species are famous for their **symbiotic**, or cooperative, relationships with ants. This means that both species get something good out of the deal. Aphids, for example, feed on sugary plants and produce a waste, called honeydew, that ants love. To an ant, an aphid is like a cow. The ants keep watch over herds of aphids and milk them by stroking them with their antennae. In the fall, the ants carry aphid eggs to their nests and care for them through the winter. This way the ants will have a fresh herd in the spring. The ants get fed and the aphids are protected from predators and saved from freezing, so everybody's happy.

Aphids are definitely not a plant's best friend, but many other hemipterans are used by farmers and gardeners to get rid of plant pests. Minute pirate bugs, for example, are tiny predators that eat aphids and dozens of other crop-damaging pests, like spider mites, whiteflies, and weevils. Plant-feeding thrips are their favorite meal, and the pirate bugs can often be spotted walking around with a thrip or two stuck on their beaks.

Hemipterans are the only insects you might see bobbing on the surface of the ocean. Sea skaters are a type of water strider. They spend their entire lives at sea, walking on the water's surface and living on bits of floating algae. Most hemipterans, however, are terrestrial. Look for them on plants around your home.

DID YOU KNOW?
Red-eyed froghopper nymphs, called spittlebugs, ooze a liquid that they whip into a foam. The foam looks like a big blob of spit. It protects them when they're feeding.

17-Year Cicada

Magicicada cassini

SAY IT! *MA-jih-sih-KAY-dah kuh-SEE-nee*

Although some cicadas have one life cycle every year, adults of the *Magicicada* genus appear only every 13 or 17 years, depending on the species. These cicadas spend most of their lives feeding on roots underground. When they emerge for their final molt, *Magicicada cassini* nymphs leave millions of empty shells stuck on trees. The males of this species often sing together in one very loud chorus—making enough noise to drive away birds and other predators.

INSECT STATS

Habitat

Forests of the United States

Length

1 to 1½ inches

Color/Pattern

Black body with orange wings and legs; red eyes

Diet

NYMPH: Plant roots
ADULT: Small twigs

Life Span

NYMPH: 17 years
ADULT: 5 to 6 weeks

Hibiscus Harlequin Bug (or Cotton Harlequin Bug)

Tectocoris diophthalmus

SAY IT! *Tek-TOK-or-us dye-oh-THAL-mus*

The hibiscus harlequin bug is one of many species of jewel bugs—named for their brilliant colors and patterns—found throughout the world. Hibiscus harlequin females lay about 150 pink, barrel-shaped eggs, which they wrap around beach hibiscus stems. They stand guard over their eggs and fiercely protect them from predators.

INSECT STATS

Habitat

Coasts of Australia, New Guinea, and several Pacific Islands

Length

½ to 1 inch (males are larger than females)

Color/Pattern

FEMALE: Orange, with metallic blue patches

MALE: Red or blue, with metallic patches of blue or green

Diet

Sap of hibiscus flowers and cotton plants

Life Span

ADULT: 3 to 4 months

Oak Treehopper

Platycotis vittata

SAY IT! *Pla-tee-KO-tis vih-TAH-tay*

Butterflies aren't the only beauty queens in the insect world. Treehoppers are often brightly colored, with interesting body shapes. The oak treehopper is one of more than 3,000 species of treehoppers. Some treehoppers are called thorn bugs, because they have a large triangular thorax, called a helmet, that rises to a sharp tip. These tips look like thorns on a rose stem. Helmets come in many shapes. The Brazilian treehopper's helmet looks like it has helicopter blades tipped with balls.

INSECT STATS

Habitat	Diet
Oak trees, from Canada to Brazil	Sap of oak trees
Length	**Life Span**
About ½ inch	**ADULT:** 3 to 4 months
Color/Pattern	
Grayish-blue or turquoise body with red and gold stripes	

Common Water Strider

Aquarius remigis

SAY IT! *Ah-KWAIR-ih-us REE-my-gees*

Although they look like ordinary bugs, water striders have a superpower. They can walk on water! The secret is their hairy legs. Thousands of leg hairs capture microscopic bubbles of air. The bubbles allow the bug to float and skate across the water's surface. Water striders' long middle and back legs are used to paddle and steer. These insects move so fast that you would have to swim 400 miles an hour to match their speed.

INSECT STATS

Habitat

Ponds, lakes, and slow-moving streams in North America

Length

About ½ inch

Color/Pattern

Dark brown or black, with silvery-white stripes along each side

Diet

Mosquito larvae and other insects

Life Span

ADULT: Up to 1 year

JUNIOR SCIENTISTS IN ACTION

If you've ever done a "sink or float" experiment, you know that metal sinks. Or does it?

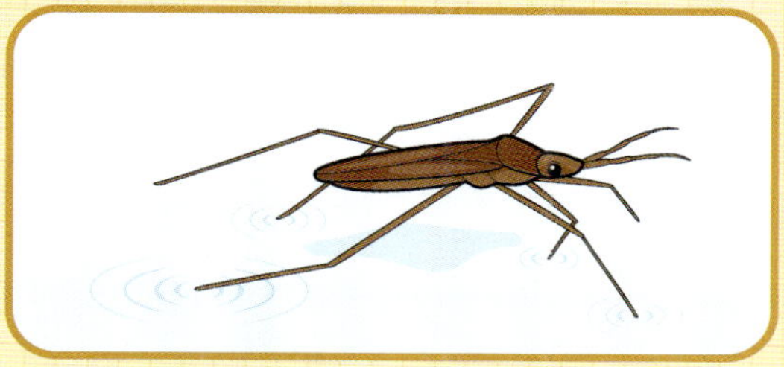

TEST IT

Fill a small glass or bowl with water. Carefully lay a paper clip on top of the water. It floats! But why?

HOW DOES IT WORK?

Water is a mixture of two gases—hydrogen and oxygen. Every molecule of water contains two hydrogen atoms and one oxygen atom—which you might know as the formula H_2O. Water molecules hold on tightly to one another, especially on the surface. This is called surface tension, and it acts like a thin skin that can keep objects from sinking. Like the paper clip, water striders use surface tension—and their air-covered hairy legs—to walk across water.

TRY THIS

Let's play with surface tension! How many drops of water do you think would fit on top of a penny? Using an eyedropper, place one drop of water at a time on a penny. How many drops can you add before the penny overflows?

Orthoptera: Insects That Chirp, Jump, and Fly

If humans could jump the way orthopterans do, we'd be able to leap the length of a football field! There are four main groups in the Orthoptera order: grasshoppers, crickets, katydids, and locusts. They have large hind legs with special knee joints that act as springs. These legs can send them forward up to 20 times their body length.

The 20,000 species of Orthoptera also have leathery front wings, called tegmina. The tegmina protect the softer back wings, which are folded up like fans beneath them. Most orthopterans are able to jump *and* fly. This makes it easy for these insect athletes to escape predators.

In addition to jumping, grasshoppers and crickets are both famous for chirping, but they make their sounds in different ways. Grasshoppers, which are active during the day, make sounds by rubbing their legs against their wings. Crickets, which are active at night, rub their wings together. Grasshoppers are herbivores, which means they eat only plants. Crickets are omnivores and eat both plants and other animals. Within each group, there are a few species that cannot fly. The giant weta, a cricket relative, can be twice the size of a mouse and is so large that it can't fly or even jump!

Katydids are related to crickets. Like crickets, they "sing" by rubbing their wings together. Their chirps sound as if they're saying, "Katy-did, katy-didn't." Their green wings look just like leaves, which is a perfect disguise for living in their treetop homes. Most katydids are ½ to 2 inches long, but giant species can be 6 inches long with 20-inch wingspans. Although all katydids have wings, there are a few species, called bush crickets, that cannot fly.

Grasshoppers also have cousins, called locusts, but they're not the sort of relatives you'd want to invite to a family picnic. Although grasshoppers like to be by themselves and don't really travel far from home, migratory locusts gather in huge swarms and travel long distances. Migratory locusts are found only in Africa, Asia, Australia, and New Zealand, although the largest locust swarm ever recorded was in the United States. In 1875, trillions of Rocky Mountain locusts swooped down to the Great Plains. Laura Ingalls, future author of *Little House on the Prairie*, was nine when locusts arrived at her farm. She later wrote:

> **The rasping whirring of their wings filled the whole air and they hit the ground and the house with the noise of a hailstorm.**

The locusts left as suddenly as they came, and by 1902, they were extinct. Not a single one was left alive anywhere on Earth. Scientists today still don't know why they disappeared.

Thankfully, locust swarms are rare, and most orthopterans cause little damage to plants. Grasshoppers and crickets are a good source of food for people and animals. In many Asian cultures, they're seen as good-luck symbols. They live all over the world, but you're most likely to hear their songs during the summer months.

DID YOU KNOW?
People began keeping crickets as pets in ancient China, where they were housed in fancy golden cages and carved gourds.

House Cricket

Acheta domesticus

SAY IT! *Ah-CHEH-tah doh-MES-tih-kus*

If an insect in your bedroom is keeping you awake with its singing, it's probably a house cricket. These chirping insects were once raised to be used as fish bait and pet food, but today they are raised to be eaten by humans. A serving of crickets has more calcium than milk, more iron than spinach, more fiber than green beans, and less fat than fish. Yum!

INSECT STATS

Habitat

Fields, forests, and houses worldwide, except Antarctica

Length

Less than 1 inch

Color/Pattern

Gray or light brown

Diet

INSIDE: Clothing and other fabrics

OUTSIDE: Fungi, plants, dead animals, and insects, including other crickets

Life Span

ADULT: 2 to 3 months

Leichhardt's Grasshopper

Petasida ephippigera

SAY IT! *Peh-TAH-sih-dah ef-pih-GAIR-ah*

These fancy grasshoppers are picky eaters that feed on only minty *Pityrodia* bushes in Australia. Most Leichhardt's grasshoppers stay on a single bush for their entire lives. They hatch at the bottom of the plant and slowly work their way to the top. These grasshoppers have wings, but they don't really fly more than a few inches from their chosen bush. Aboriginal people call them *Alyurr*, meaning "children of the lightning man," because they appear at the beginning of Australia's tropical storm season.

INSECT STATS

Habitat

Tropical forests of northern Australia

Length

FEMALE: Up to 2¼ inches

MALE: Up to 1½ inches

Color/Pattern

Orange, with bright blue and red markings

Diet

Pityrodia plants

Life Span

ADULT: About 5 months

Oblong-Winged Katydid

Amblycorypha oblongifolia

SAY IT! *Am-blee-KOR-ee-fah ob-LONG-ih-fol-ee-ah*

Katydids are difficult to see because their leaflike appearance is such good camouflage. Spotting a pink katydid is almost impossible, since they are very rare in the wild. Although brightly colored katydids are hard to find in the countryside, entomologists at the Audubon Louisiana Nature Center in New Orleans were able to breed them in captivity. They kept their katydids healthy with a menu of lettuce, oats, dog food, sliced fruit, and cereal.

INSECT STATS

Habitat

Weedy areas of the eastern U.S.

Length

1½ to 2 inches

Color/Pattern

Usually green, but can also be orange, yellow, or bright pink

Diet

Mostly leaves, but will also eat fruit, pollen, nectar, and smaller insects

Life Span

ADULT: 4 to 6 months

Snowy Tree Cricket (or Thermometer Cricket)

Oecanthus fultoni

SAY IT! *Oh-KAN-thus ful-TOH-nee*

Snowy tree crickets are famous for their ability to tell the temperature. If you live in the eastern or central United States, count the number of chirps the cricket makes in 13 seconds, then add 40 to find out what the temperature is. If you live farther west, count the number of chirps in 13 seconds and add 38. Use an outdoor thermometer to record the temperature near your cricket. How accurate is your chirping thermometer?

INSECT STATS

Habitat

Trees, shrubs, and vines throughout the U.S.

Diet

Leaves and fruits, such as apples and peaches

Length

½ to ¾ inch

Life Span

ADULT: About 4 months

Color/Pattern

Light green (almost white) body with see-through light green wings

Neuroptera: Net-Winged Insects

The 5,500 species of Neuroptera live in all types of climates around the world. The four main groups—lacewings, owlflies, mantidflies, and ant lions—have some things in common with many other insect orders:

- Like dragonflies, they have wings in which both pairs are about the same size and shape.
- Like butterflies, they hold their wings up, like a tent, when they're resting.
- Like moths, their larvae spin silken cocoons.
- Like beetles, they have chewing mandibles.

So, what makes them different from dragonflies, butterflies, moths, and beetles?

It's those lacy wings! The name Neuroptera means "nerve-winged," but the wing patterns of this order are made of veins, not nerves. Each wing has a single large vein that runs along the front edge and branches out into a web of smaller veins. Neuropteran larvae spin not one but two cocoons. First, they spin a loosely woven covering, like a net. Then they add a tightly woven cocoon inside.

Insect-eating neuropteran larvae have unique ways of hunting and feeding. Lacewing larvae look like tiny hairy alligators, with long bodies and jawlike pincers that clamp down on prey. They're nicknamed "aphid lions," and farmers use them to control aphids and other pesky plant pests. Mantidfly larvae hitch a ride on the back of a wolf spider and eat the eggs in the spider's egg sac. Ant lion larvae are the most dedicated hunters. They're often called doodlebugs, because of the trails they leave in soft sandy soil. But don't let the cute name fool you. They are ferocious, sneaky predators that build pit traps to capture ant snacks.

Doodlebugs have been the subject of folktales around the world. Many countries have chants that are supposed to bring the doodlebug out of its trap. In *The Adventures of Tom Sawyer*, Mark Twain included this chant:

Doodlebug, doodlebug, tell me what I want to know.

Doodlebugs may come out if you chant, but it's not because of the words you say. Scientists believe that they respond to the sound vibrations caused by your voice.

You can find lacy-winged neuropterans living on trees, shrubs, and other plants. The larvae of some species are usually hidden underground, but others live in tree bark. If you spot a 2- or 3-inch-wide pile of dirt that looks like a volcano with a crater in the middle, you've found a doodlebug trap!

DID YOU KNOW?
Lacewings have special ears at the base of their wings that help them hear the high-pitched sounds made by hungry bats.

Ant Lion (or Doodlebug)

Myrmeleon

SAY IT! *Mer-MEE-lee-un*

Doodlebug pit builders capture prey with their sharp, strong mandibles. They begin building their pit by backing into the soil while flinging dirt aside and moving in a circular pattern. The finished trap is shaped like a funnel. The ant lion larva hides at the bottom of the funnel, with its jaws open. Ants that fall into the crater slide right into its waiting mouth!

INSECT STATS

Habitat

Sandy, dry areas worldwide, especially warm areas

Length

LARVA: ¼ to ½ inch

ADULT: 1½ to 2 inches

Color/Pattern

Brown, with clear wings and long clubbed antennae

Diet

LARVA: Mostly ants

ADULT: Nectar, pollen, some insects

Life Span

LARVA: 1 to 2 years

ADULT: 1 to 2 months

Common Green Lacewing

Chrysoperla carnea

SAY IT! *Kris-oh-PER-lah KAR-nee-ah*

More than half of all neuropterans are lacewings. They range in size from small dustywings less than one-tenth of an inch long, to large tropical species that have 6-inch wingspans. Lacewing larvae of some species are nicknamed "junk bugs" because they carry bits of leaves, sand, and insect shells on their backs as camouflage.

INSECT STATS

Habitat

Grasses and shrubs in the Northern Hemisphere

Length

LARVA: About ¼ inch
ADULT: ½ to ¾ inch

Color/Pattern

Green, with see-through wings and golden eyes

Diet

LARVA: Aphids and other insect pests
ADULT: Nectar, pollen, honeydew

Life Span

LARVA: 2 to 3 weeks
ADULT: 4 to 6 weeks

Macaronius Owlfly

Libelloides macaronius

SAY IT! *Lye-bel-OH-ih-deez mak-ah-ROH-nee-us*

What has wings like a dragonfly, the bright colors and long clubbed antennae of a butterfly, and the thick body of a moth? It's an owlfly! Most owlflies have yellow markings on their bodies, but the macaronius owlfly is the most colorful species. Owlflies are the strongest neuropteran fliers. They are so strong that they can catch an insect while flying. Owlfly larvae look like doodlebugs, but they hide in dried leaves and on trees to surprise their prey.

INSECT STATS

Habitat	Diet
Meadows and pine forests in Europe	Insects
Length	**Life Span**
ADULT: 1 to 1½ inches	Limited information available; most likely 3 to 4 months
Color/Pattern	
Fat black body with yellow-and-black wings; long clubbed antennae; large eyes	

Wasp Mantidfly

Climaciella brunnea

SAY IT! *Kligh-mah-see-EL-ah BRUN-ee-ah*

This insect has a very confusing name. The wasp mantidfly is not a wasp, a mantis, or a fly. All mantidflies have the triangle-shaped head and long front legs of a praying mantis and the large bulging eyes of a housefly. Wasp mantidflies also have striped abdomens like wasps. Although they look strange and fearsome, mantidflies don't have stingers and are harmless to humans.

INSECT STATS

Habitat

Fields and meadows in North America, Mexico, and Central America

Length

ADULT: About 1 inch

Color/Pattern

Dark brown and yellow

Diet

LARVA: Spider eggs, especially wolf spiders

ADULT: Insects, as well as nectar and sap

Life Span

3 to 4 months, from late spring to summer

FACTS TO DRIVE YOU BUGGY

Green lacewings and stinkbugs belong to two different orders, but they have one thing in common: They stink! To understand *why*, here's a quick chemistry lesson.

Everything that you see, eat, touch, drink, or eat is made of substances called **elements**. Your body, for example, contains oxygen, carbon, hydrogen, and about two dozen other elements. When elements are combined, they produce odors, or smells. The elements of cookies baking in the oven smell great, but the elements in spoiled milk create a not-so-great odor.

Lacewings and other smelly bugs create stinky odors in the same way. They shoot out their chemical mixtures when they feel like they are in danger. They also use scents to communicate. One blend that stinkbugs make sends out a message to other members of the colony: *Hey! I've found a great place to live!* The more stink they make, the more of their friends show up.

Many insects have unusual smells. The western conifer seed bug smells like pine needles mixed with turpentine. Roaches have an oily smell. Other insects make nice odors. Admiral butterflies smell like wintergreen. Citronella ants smell like lemons. When honeybees send out a danger warning, it smells like bananas!

MORE TO DISCOVER

BOOKS

Bugs A to Z by Caroline Lawton
Larger-than-life photos and interesting facts about dozens of insects make this the perfect book for beginning entomologists.

Eat-a-Bug Cookbook by David George Gordon
Become an insect chef or learn how to grow your own insects with this cookbook, which includes colorful photos of buggy recipes.

Ultimate Bugopedia by Darlyne Murawski and Nancy Honovich
Learn oodles of interesting bug facts with this colorful book from National Geographic Kids.

WEBSITES

Go Buggy for Bugs!
Play online games, watch videos, create crafts, and read e-books at pestworldforkids.org.

Grow a Garden
Turn your butterfly garden into a wildlife habitat. Find out how at nwf .org/garden-for-wildlife.

Grow Your Own Insects
Insect Lore is a company that makes insect-growing kits, such as Butterfly Garden and Ladybug Land. They allow you to watch larvae transform into pupae and adults. Available from insectlore.com, Amazon, and school supply stores.

Mealworm Madness!

Purchase live mealworms at any pet store, then investigate mealworm behavior with more than 20 super science experiments at mealwormsadventuring.weebly.com/experiments.html.

Watch Them Waggle!

Watch an awesome YouTube video about honeybees, produced by the Smithsonian and narrated by David Attenborough. Visit youtube.com and search for the title "What's the Waggle Dance? And Why Do Honeybees Do It?"

What's That Bug?

Having trouble identifying an insect? Try this online identification tool powered by the Raid Entomology Lab at raid.com/en-us/bug-id.

GLOSSARY

ADAPTATION (a-dap-TAY-shun): *A change in a creature that makes it able to survive in its environment.* Migration and camouflage are types of animal **adaptations**.

ARTHROPOD (AR-throh-pod): *Any animal with an exoskeleton, a body made of segments or parts, and jointed legs*. Insects, spiders, and lobsters are **arthropods**.

CHITIN (KY-ten): *The material from which an exoskeleton is made.* An insect's outer covering is made of **chitin**.

CHRYSALIS (KRIS-uh-lis): *The pupa stage of a butterfly. Also, the hard outer covering of a butterfly pupa.* A caterpillar attaches its **chrysalis** to a leaf or twig.

COCOON (kuh-KOON): *The silky covering spun by moths and other types of insect larvae before entering the pupa stage*. Moths, fleas, and many other insects spin **cocoons** to protect themselves as they transform from a pupa to an adult.

COLONY (COL-uh-nee): *A group or community of a single species living together.* Some termite **colonies** have one million or more members.

CRUSTACEAN (kruhs-TAY-shun): *An arthropod that, typically, spends most of its time in the water, such as a lobster, crab, or shrimp.* Most **crustaceans** live in or near water.

DECOMPOSER (dee-com-POH-ser): *Organisms that break down dead plants and animals.* Bacteria, fungi, some insects, and snails are **decomposers**.

ECOSYSTEM (EE-koh-sis-tem): *The interaction of living organisms and environmental factors such as sun, wind, and rain, within a specific location. A subdivision of a biome.* The Amazon rain forest is an **ecosystem** of the forest biome. The Sahara is a desert **ecosystem**.

ELEMENT (EL-ih-ment): *Any material that cannot be broken down into other materials.* Oxygen is one of the most common **elements** on Earth.

ENTOMOLOGIST (en-toh-MAHL-oh-jist): *A scientist who studies insects.* Most **entomologists** study one type or one group of insects.

EXOSKELETON (ek-sow-SKEH-luh-tun): *The hard outer shell of an insect or other animal.* Insects, spiders, and crabs have **exoskeletons** instead of bones.

GENES (JEENZ): *Microscopic parts of cells that make you who you are and what you look like.* A dog has **genes** that make it a dog instead of a cat or a bird.

INVERTEBRATE (in-VER-teh-brayt): *An animal that does not have a backbone.* Insects, worms, and jellyfish are **invertebrates**.

LENS (LENZ): *The clear part of the eye that focuses light to form images.* Compound eyes are made of many **lenses**.

LIFE CYCLE (lyf SIGH-kul): *The stages that living things go through during their lifetimes.* Insects may have three or four stages in their **life cycles**.

MANDIBLES (MAN-dih-buls): *The two mouthparts of an insect.* The **mandibles** of a dobsonfly can be twice the length of its head.

METAMORPHOSIS (met-ah-MOHR-fah-sis): *The multistep process insects go through to develop from an egg to an adult.* Butterfly **metamorphosis** includes an egg, a larva, a pupa, and an adult stage.

MIGRATE (MY-grayt): *To move from one area or climate to another.* Some dragonflies **migrate** more than 2,000 miles to mate.

MOLTING (MOHLT-ing): *To shed an old outer layer in order to grow.* Grasshopper nymphs **molt** five to six times before they become adults.

OOTHECA (oh-ah-THEE-kah): *The egg case of cockroaches, mantises, and some other insects.* An **ootheca** usually begins as a foam, then hardens into a protective shell.

PHEROMONE (FEHR-uh-mohn): *A chemical that an animal makes to communicate with other animals, usually of the same species.* Yellow jacket wasps make a **pheromone** that tells other yellow jackets to attack.

POLLINATED (PAH-luh-nayt-ed): *To move pollen from one plant to another of the same species so new seeds can form.* More than one-third of the world's food crops depend on bees and other animals to **pollinate** their plants.

PREDATOR (PREH-dah-tohr): *An animal that kills and eats other animals.* **Predator** wasps feed on many types of insects and spiders.

PROBOSCIS (proh-BAHS-kis): *A long mouthpart that is shaped like a flexible tube.* A butterfly has a coiled **proboscis**.

SPECIES (SPEE-seez): *A group of living things that has many characteristics in common and can mate to make others of their kind.* A monarch butterfly cannot mate with a luna moth because they are two different **species**.

SYMBIOTIC (sim-bye-AH-tik): *The relationship between two different living things that helps both survive.* Ants and aphids both get good things from their **symbiotic** partnership.

TAXONOMY (tax-AH-noh-mee): *A scientific system of grouping living things, such as animals or plants, using the characteristics they have in common.* Carl Linnaeus's **taxonomy** of plants earned him the title of "the Father of Modern Botany."

TERRESTRIAL (ter-RES-tree-ul): *A way of describing things that live on land.* Beetles, elephants, and humans are **terrestrial**.

INDEX

ABOUT THE AUTHOR

SHARMAN JOHNSTON, EdD, is a lifelong educator who believes that reading is the key that unlocks the door to adventure, wonder, and school success. She has worked with thousands of teachers across the United States, teaching them ways to inspire a love of books with the use of interactive activities that extend and enrich learning. Internationally, Dr. Johnston has spoken at the worldwide headquarters of the Association Montessori Internationale in Amsterdam and participated in a panel discussion concerning global children's issues at the United Nations in Geneva.

Today, "Dr. J" spends most of her time creating activity books and other resources designed to help young children understand and explore the world around them. Her science materials cover everything from astronomy to zoology. Multicultural education is one of her favorite topics, and she has developed hundreds of resources that introduce children to countries and cultures around the world.

Dr. J lives on a lake in East Texas, surrounded by forests—and lots of insects!